A Reason for Handwriting
Student Worktext

Cursive D

EAN#: 978-0-936785-42-4
ISBN#: 0-936785-42-X
TL#: HWSWTD2023WC

Published by Concerned Communications, LLC
P.O. Box 1000 • Siloam Springs, AR 72761

Authors	**Carol Ann Retzer**
	Eva Hoshino
Proofreaders	**Daniel Swatsenberg**
	Marcie Smith
Layout	**Mark Decker**
	Melissa Habermas
Illustrations	**Rob Harrell**
Colorists	**Josh & Aimee Ray**

Scripture translation selected for appropriate vocabulary level.
All verses are taken from *The Living Bible*, Tyndale House Publishers,
Wheaton, Illinois 60187. Used by permission.

Please, Help Us Hold Down Costs!

Photocopy machines are wonderful inventions, but did you know that it's ILLEGAL to reproduce copyrighted material?

Years of work and hundreds of thousands of dollars have gone into the development and production of **A Reason For Handwriting**®. Only your Christian integrity can help us avoid unnecessary price increases due to ILLEGAL photocopying.

Thank you for honoring copyright laws and not yielding to the temptation to "run off a few copies." It's not cost effective and it's ILLEGAL as well!

Attention Parents & Teachers:

Don't Settle for HALF a Curriculum!

A Reason For Handwriting® **Student Worktexts** integrate faith and learning by featuring lessons based on Scripture verses and built-in opportunities for sharing God's Word with others.

But, the **A Reason For Handwriting**® curriculum offers much, much more!

The **Comprehensive K-6th Teacher Guidebook** is full of essential instructions, helpful tips, and teacher-tested techniques to help you make the most of your handwriting practice.

Key instructional information in the **Teacher Guidebook** includes:

- **The Suggested Weekly Schedule**
- **Daily Lesson Plans**
- **Tips for Teaching Cursive Handwriting**
- **Techniques for Grading**

Plus the **Teacher Guidebook** includes a wealth of teacher-tested tips and enrichment ideas:

- **A Comprehesive Skills Index**
- **Extended Activities**
- **Ways to Share Border Sheets**
- **Letter Formation Charts**
- **Tips for Proper Positioning**
- **Letter Group Charts**
- **Vocabulary Lists**
- **Common Handwriting Problems**
- **Black Line Masters**

To order the **A Reason For Handwriting**® **K-6th Teacher Guidebook** that goes with this **Student Worktext**, contact your curriculum supplier or call 800.447.4332

Or go to:
www.AReasonFor.com

Just For Kids!

Welcome to A Reason For Handwriting®

This year you'll learn to write better, memorize Scripture, share God's Word, and have FUN!

Each week you'll practice letters and groups of letters from a different Scripture verse. Then you'll write the entire verse on practice paper. At the end of each week you'll pick a Scripture Border Sheet from the back of your Worktext,

Parker

Susan

Rodney

write the verse in your very best handwriting, and use your creative talents to color and decorate it. Now comes the really FUN part: Sharing God's Word!

You can share God's Word, in your very own handwriting, by giving people your finished Scripture Border Sheets! You can take them to nursing homes, share them with friends, make placemats for your kitchen table, mail them to someone who isn't feeling well. . . you get the idea. And we're sure you'll come up with even more ideas throughout the year!

And sharing God's Word with others gives you the very best reason for improving your handwriting!

Meet New Friends

Throughout this book, you'll see illustrations of kids like you who are caring, sharing, working, and learning. Be sure to watch for these new faces!

Rachel

Greg

Jared

Kes

Alli

How to Become A Five Star Student!

Do you want your writing to look its very best? Here are the five basic areas you should consider when evaluating your handwriting form:

 Alignment

Each letter or word should sit on the line, not above or below it.

Slant

The letter slant should be uniform and consistent. (To help you determine slant, draw a top-to-bottom line straight down the middle of each letter in a sentence.)

 Size

Capital letters are all one full space tall. The lowercase letters *b, d, f, h, k, l,* and *t* are also one space tall. All other lowercase letters are half-a-space tall. Also, any letter that goes below the line should extend for half a space.

 Shape

Letters should be consistent and easy to read. Minor differences from the model are okay, but all your letters must be formed with the proper strokes to avoid developing bad habits.

 Spacing

Letters should be clearly identifiable. They should not run into each other, or be too far apart. Each word should be separated from the next word. Remember, a little more space is needed between sentences than between words.

Follow these guidelines, focusing on consistency and quality, and you'll be a Five Star student!

The following practice sentence contains all the letters of the alphabet:

God created zebras and foxes to walk, jump, and hide very quickly.

To The Teacher

Before beginning instruction, please review the
Weekly Lesson Format (Teacher Guidebook, page 56).
Here you will find detailed directions for implementing
the 5-day format, as well as suggestions for using the
Scripture Border Sheets.

Careful review of this material at the start of the school year
will greatly enhance the effectiveness of this curriculum.

Name _____

TIP OF THE WEEK

Look for punctuation in this week's verse.
An exclamation mark follows a word or words that show strong
feelings; a colon indicates a pause. Watch for the period and semi-colon, too.

Day One   Practice the following letters and words from this week's Scripture.

Rr

read

store

worry

Day Two   Continue practicing letters and words from this week's Scripture.

Hh

Heavenly

They

food

Un

valuable

than

feeds

Day Four   Practice this week's entire Scripture verse by tracing over each of the words below.

Look at the birds! They don't
worry about what to eat—they
don't need to sow or reap or store
up food—for your Heavenly Father
feeds them. And you are far more
valuable to Him than they are.

Matthew 6:26

FOR DISCUSSION
What sort of things do you worry about? Can
trusting God help you deal with your problems?
Explain.

Name_____

TIP OF THE WEEK

The lowercase *g* begins with the same
overstroke as the letters *m*, *n*, *v*, *x*, and *y*.
Be sure to spend some time practicing this group of letters.

Day One Practice the following letters and words from this week's Scripture.

Gg

grudge

praying

holding

Day Two Continue practicing letters and words from this week's Scripture.

Zz
citizen

against

heaven

Ff

Father

first

forgive

Day Four Practice this week's entire Scripture verse by tracing over each of the words below.

When you are praying, first forgive anyone you are holding a grudge against, so that your Father in heaven will forgive you your sins too.

Mark 11:25

FOR DISCUSSION

When someone holds a grudge, how does it make them feel inside? If you're upset with someone, what might you do to change the situation?

The lowercase tall letters, *h* and *k*, can
easily be mistaken for each other if not written clearly.
This week, focus on writing these two important letters correctly.

Day One   Practice the following letters and words from this week's Scripture.

Uu

When

away

secrets

Day Two   Continue practicing letters and words from this week's Scripture.

Uu

yourself

shut

behind

Kk

knows

reward

secretly

Day Four   **Practice this week's entire Scripture verse by tracing over each of the words below.**

When you pray, go away by yourself, all alone, and shut the door behind you and pray to your Father secretly, and your Father, who knows your secrets, will reward you.

Matthew 6:6

FOR DISCUSSION

Why is praying important? Are there different kinds of prayers? Explain.

Name _____

Tip of the week

What was the name of the town where Jesus was born? (Hint: look up Luke 2:11.) You will write that name this week as you practice the capital *B*.

Day One Practice the following letters and words from this week's Scripture.

Tt

The

greatest

shown

Day Two Continue practicing letters and words from this week's Scripture.

Bb

Bethlehem

obey

friends

Day Three — Practice the final letters and words from this week's Scripture.

P p

person

down

lays

Day Four — Practice this week's entire Scripture verse by tracing over each of the words below.

The greatest love is shown when a person lays down his life for his friends; and you are My friends if you obey Me.

— John 15:13, 14

FOR DISCUSSION

Jesus gave His life to save us. How does that make you feel? What does He ask us to do to show that we are His friends?

62

TIP OF THE WEEK

Spacing your words and letters properly is as
important to readability as is correct letter formation. As you
write your words this week, be sure to leave a letter space between them.

Day One Practice the following letters and words from this week's Scripture.

Cc

cheer

peace

overcome

Day Two Continue practicing letters and words from this week's Scripture.

Ll

trials

world

many

Day Three — Practice the final letters and words from this week's Scripture.

Hh

Here

have

earth

Day Four — Practice this week's entire Scripture verse by tracing over each of the words below.

I have told you all this so that you will have peace of heart and mind. Here on earth you will have many trials and sorrows; but cheer up, for I have overcome the world.

John 16:33

FOR DISCUSSION

What kinds of "trials and sorrows" have you had this year? How has your relationship with God helped you through?

64

Name_____

TIP OF THE WEEK

The capitals *M* and *N* are part of a much larger
family of canestroke letters (*H, K, M, N, U, V, W, X,
Y,* and *Z*). Take time this week to practice these capital letters.

Day One   Practice the following letters and words from this week's Scripture.

Nn

No

Instead

enter

Day Two   Continue practicing letters and words from this week's Scripture.

Mm

lamp

room

lampstand

Oo

one

to

who

No one lights a lamp and hides it! Instead, he puts it on a lampstand to give light to all who enter the room.

Luke 11:33

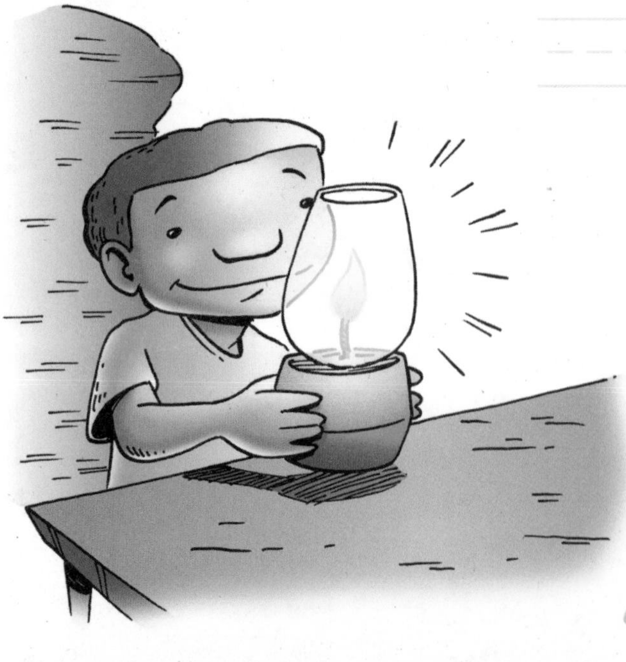

FOR DISCUSSION
What kind of light is this verse talking about? How can you "hide" the light? List some ways to share God's love with others.

Consistent letter size is very important.
It helps make your writing readable! Take extra care
this week to make sure the size of your letters is consistent.

Day One Practice the following letters and words from this week's Scripture.

Ss

man's

speech

is

Day Two Continue practicing letters and words from this week's Scripture.

Ee

treasures

filled

within

Day Three — Practice the final letters and words from this week's Scripture.

Vv

venom

reveals

evil-hearted

Day Four — Practice this week's entire Scripture verse by tracing over each of the words below.

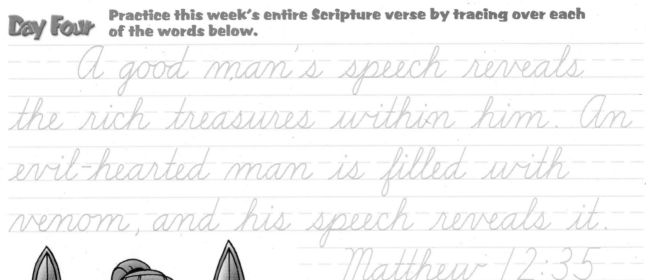

A good man's speech reveals the rich treasures within him. An evil-hearted man is filled with venom, and his speech reveals it.
Matthew 12:35

FOR DISCUSSION

How does the way you talk about others show what you're like inside? Give some examples. What does *your* speech say about *you*?

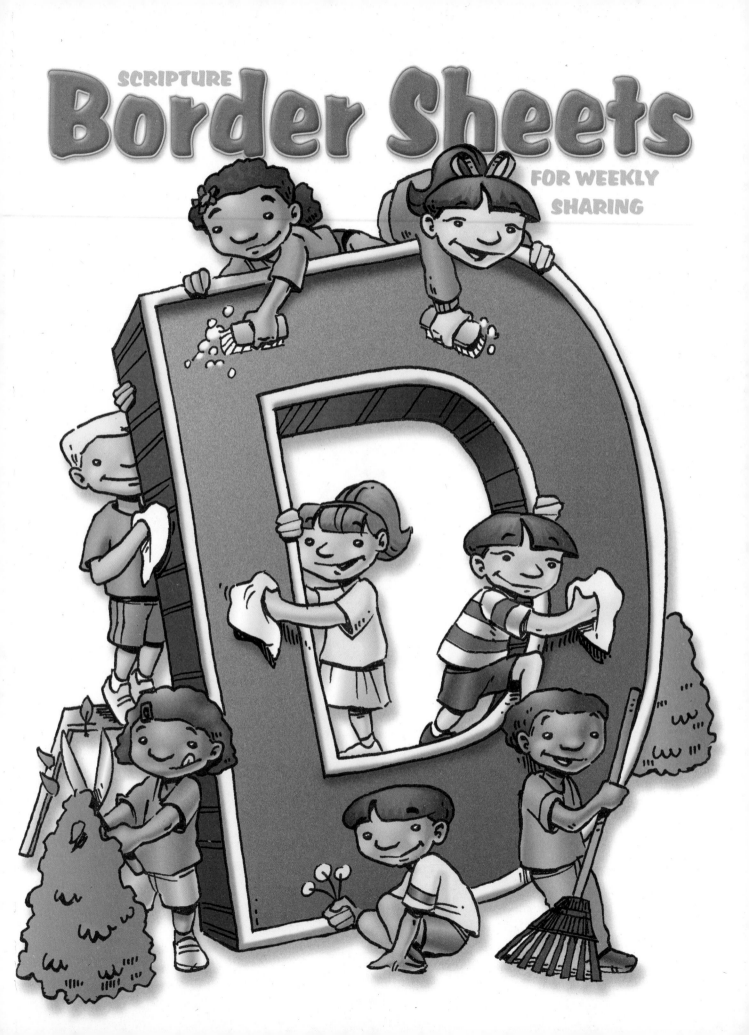

To The Teacher

The following pages are for use on Day 5 of the
Weekly Lesson Format (Teacher Guidebook, page 56).

These Scripture Border Sheets not only provide a
significant outreach component, but a strong
motivational tool as well.

This section contains 35 Scripture Border Sheets —
one per lesson, plus three blanks (pages 139, 141, and 143)
that allow for student-designed artwork.

For creative ways to use the Scripture Border Sheets
see "Ways to Share" (Teacher Guidebook, page 58).

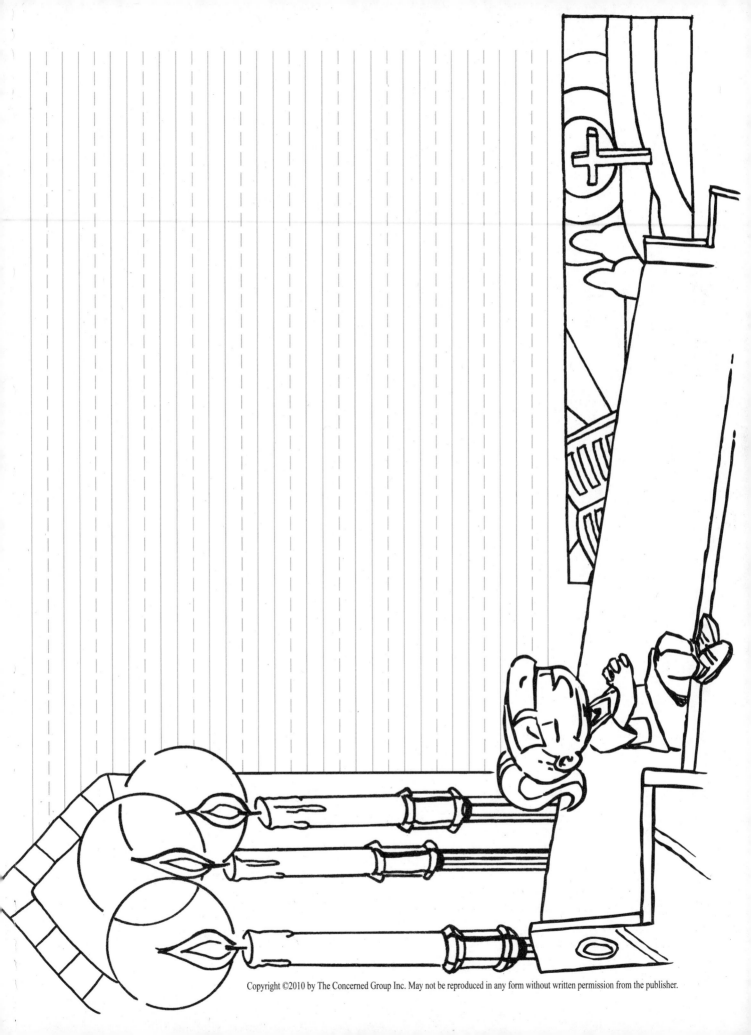

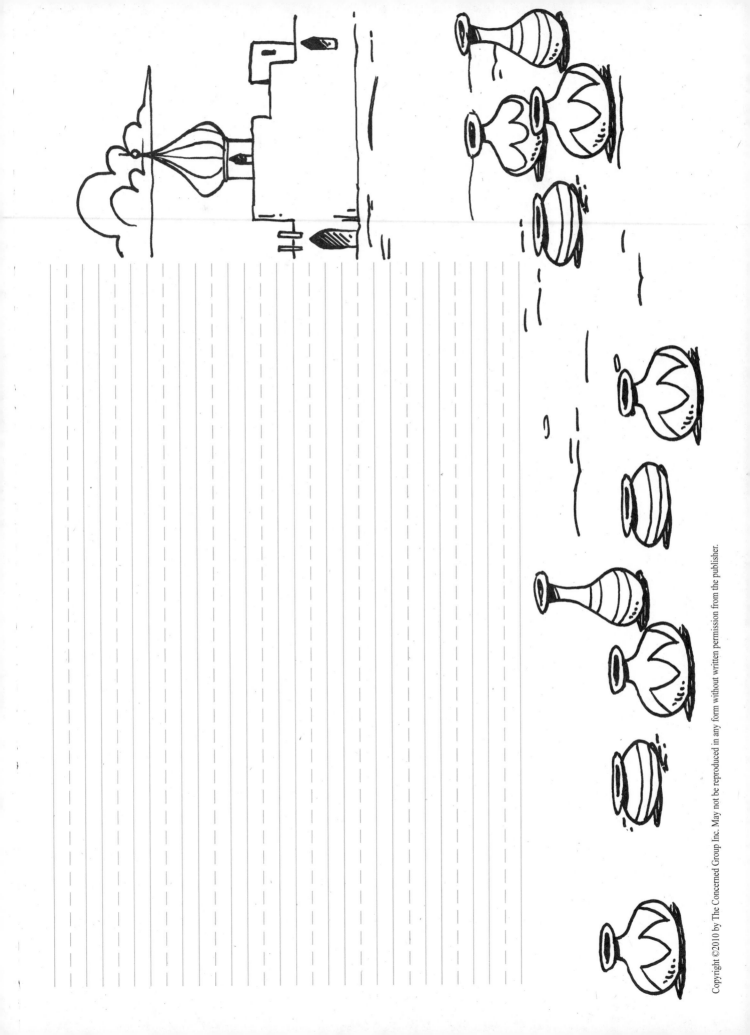

Copyright ©2010 by The Concerned Group Inc. May not be reproduced in any form without written permission from the publisher.

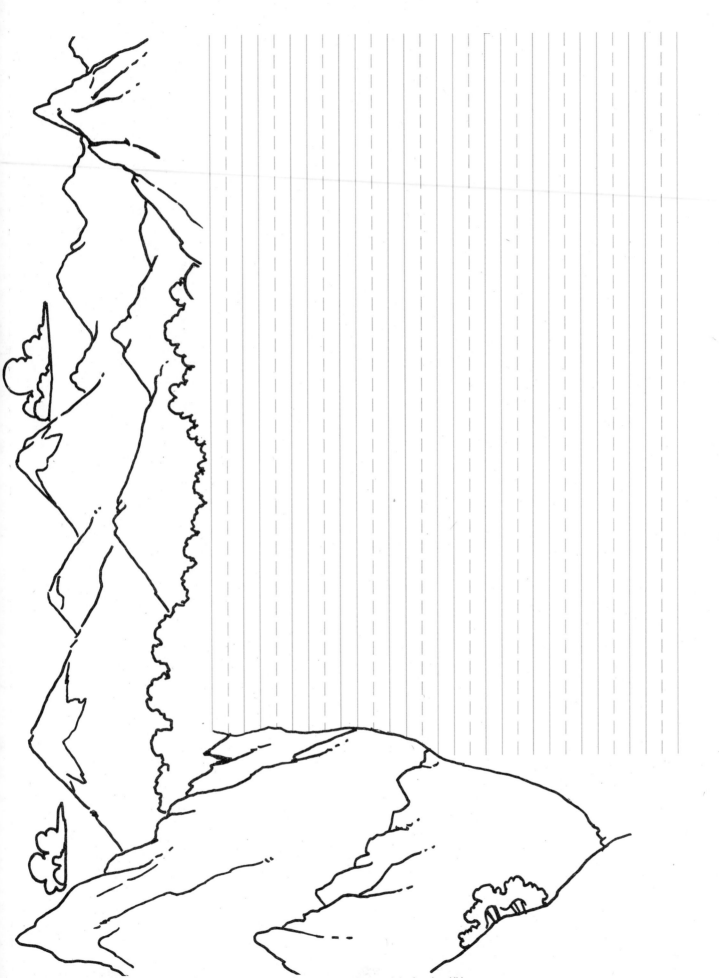

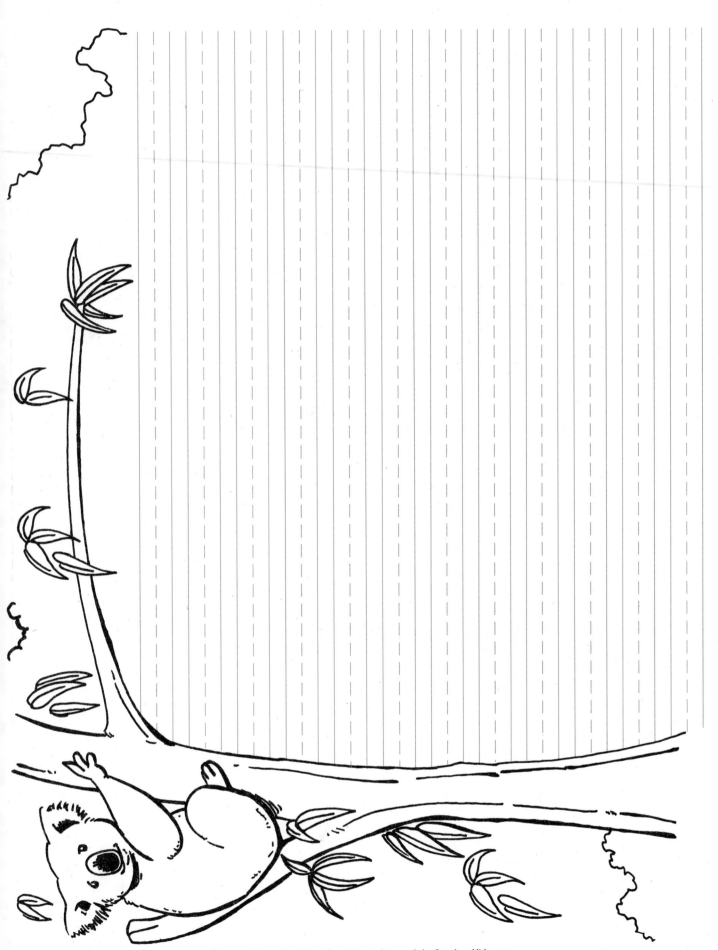

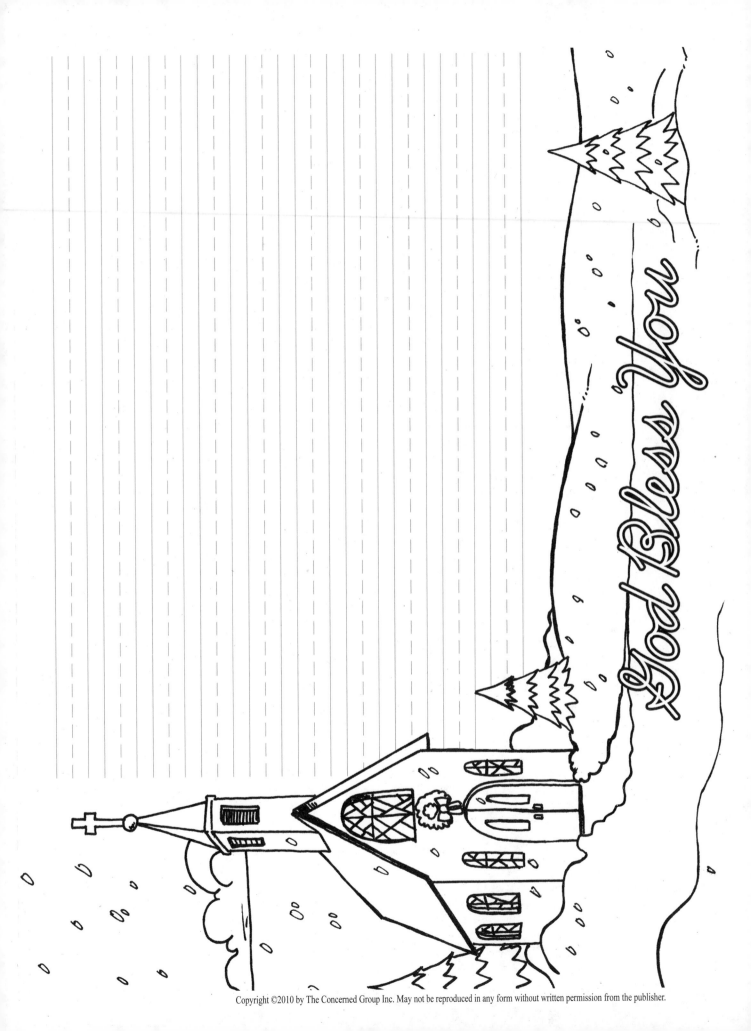

God Bless You

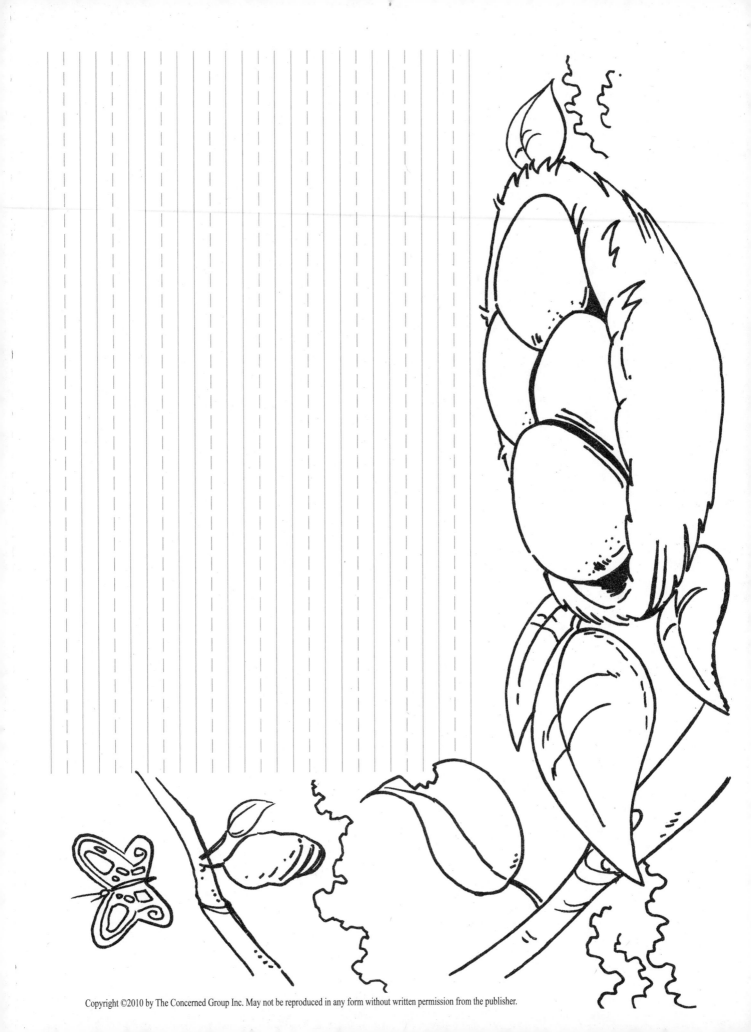

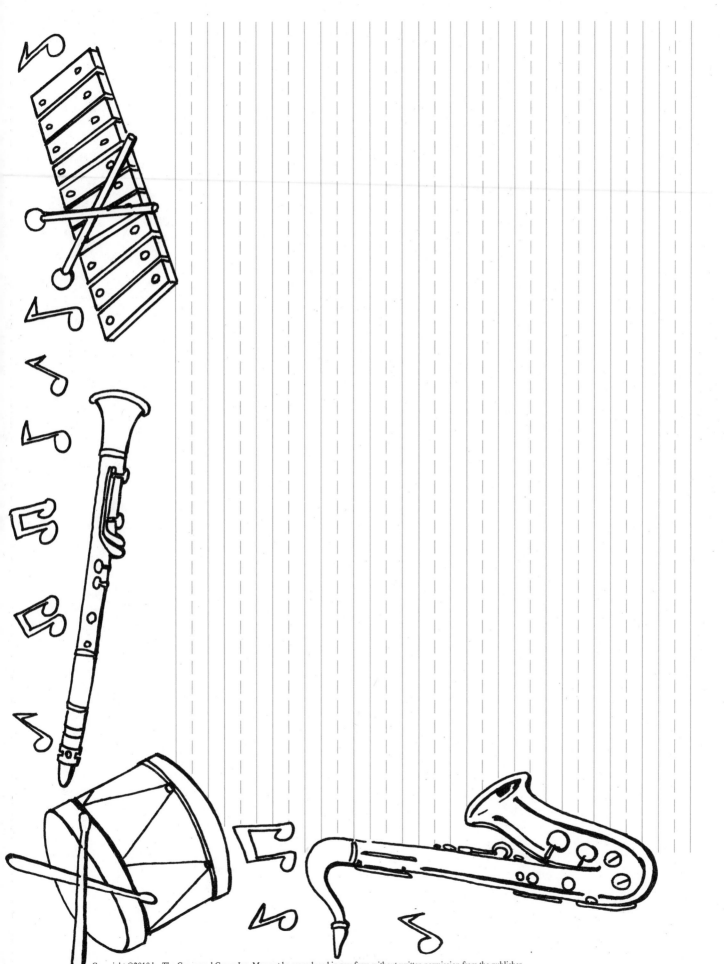

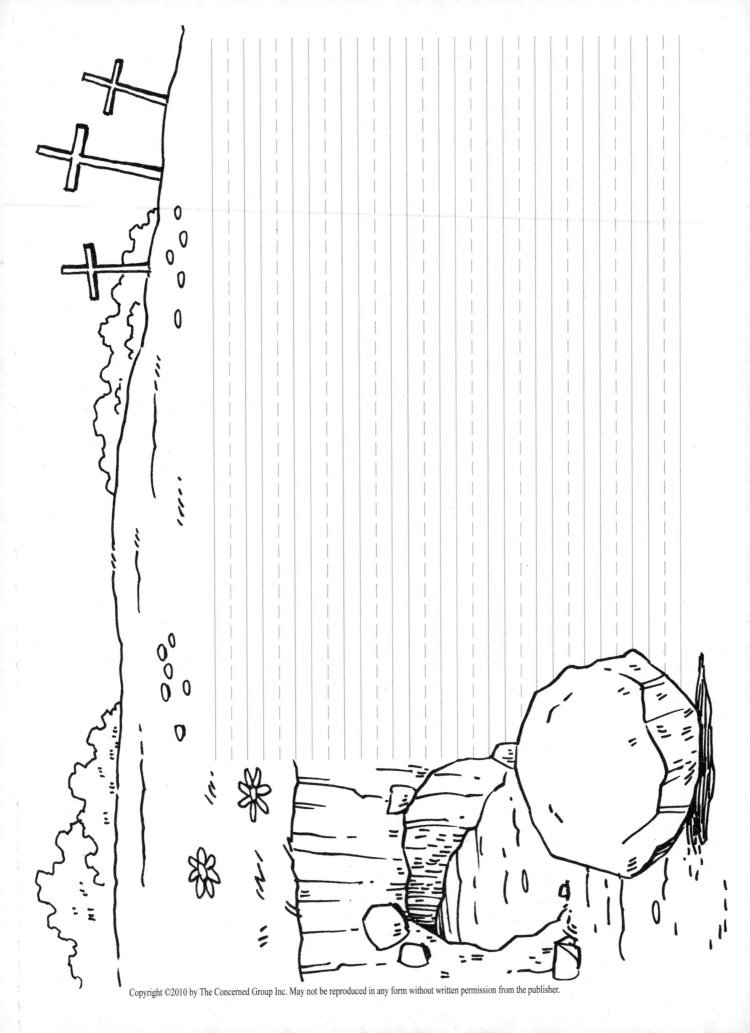

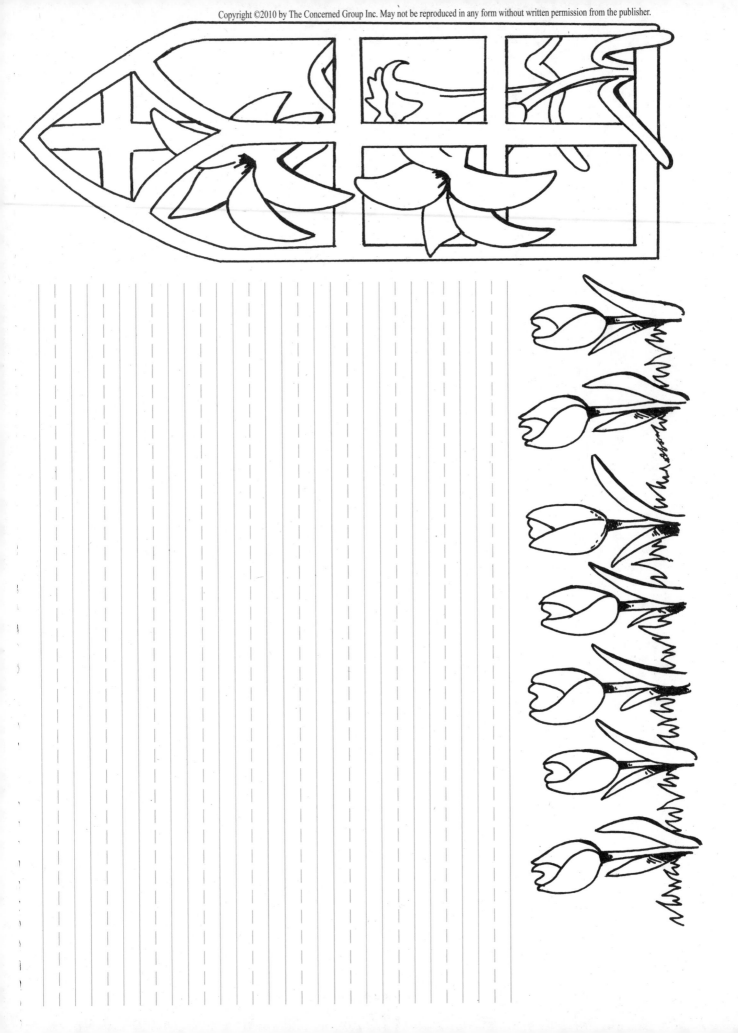

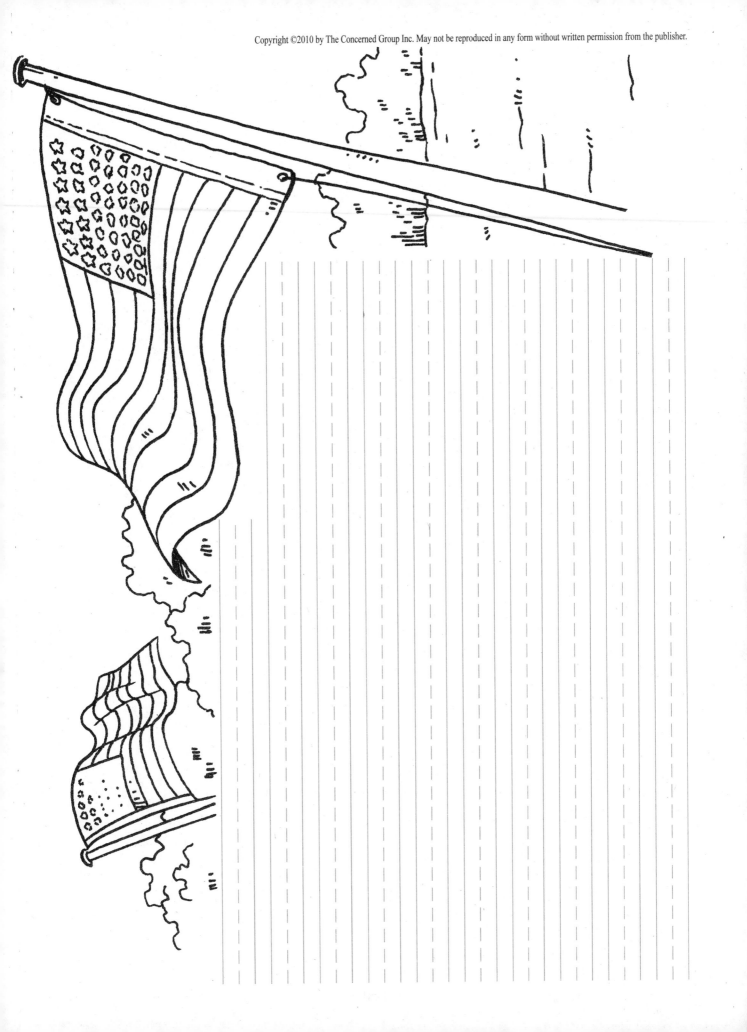